THE CANADA GOOSE

With its black neck and white cheek patch, the Canada Goose is easy to recognize.

TABLE OF CONTENTS

Photography by Lionnel Mascarenhas

Canada Geese are found across much of North America.

The correct name is Canada Goose, not Canadian Goose.

They glide smoothly across lakes, ponds, and wetlands.

Although they may seem calm, Canada Geese stay alert to danger.

DID YOU KNOW?

A group of geese on the ground is sometimes called a gaggle.

Their sharp eyes help them spot movement from far away.

A Canada Goose can have a wingspan over 5 feet (1.5 meters) across.

Their loud honking helps flocks communicate.

DID YOU KNOW?

Canada Geese are herbivores.

Built for Life

The Canada Goose uses its webbed feet to move smoothly through water and mud.

Layers of feathers help protect the goose from wind and rain.

Soft down feathers help keep the goose warm during cold weather.

Canada Geese replace old feathers with new ones during a process called molting.

Strong legs help geese walk across grass, shorelines, and wetlands.

A long neck helps the goose reach food on land and underwater.

The goose uses its bill to pull up grass and aquatic plants.

Wide wings help the goose soar through the sky.

Eyes on the sides of the head help the Canada Goose watch in many directions.

The Canada Goose is built for life on land, water, and sky.

Life on the Water

The Canada Goose spends much of its life near water.

Gliding quietly across the water, the Canada Goose moves with ease.

To reach tasty plants underwater, the Canada Goose tips upside down.

With webbed feet and waterproof feathers, geese are excellent swimmers.

Tiny ripples spread across the pond as the goose touches the water.

With powerful wings and splashing feet, the goose skims across the water.

DID YOU KNOW?

They can sleep while floating on water.

The still pond
mirrors the goose
like glass.

Families and Relationships

Canada Geese are often seen swimming side by side.

DID YOU KNOW?

Baby geese are called goslings.

Goslings can swim soon after hatching.

Canada Geese are caring and protective parents.

From their first swim, goslings stay close to their family.

Goose Behaviors

Canada Geese
sometimes stand on
one leg to help
keep warm.

By tucking one leg close to their body, geese conserve heat.

Even while resting, a goose stays alert to danger.

With one eye closed, the Canada Goose enjoys a peaceful moment.

DID YOU KNOW?

Canada Geese have a special gland near the base of their tail that produces oil.

They spread the oil over their feathers to help keep them waterproof.

DID YOU KNOW?

Canada Geese may hiss when they feel threatened.

Sharing the Wetlands

Ducks often share ponds and wetlands with Canada Geese.

Swans and Canada Geese are often found in the same peaceful wetlands.

Turtles can sometimes be seen resting near ponds where Canada Geese swim.

Cormorants often fish in the same wetland habitats as Canada Geese.

Gulls may gather near the same shorelines and open water as Canada Geese.

Blackbirds often hide among the tall reeds surrounding Canada Goose habitats.

Great Blue Herons often hunt for fish in the same wetlands as Canada Geese.

The Great Migration

Geese take turns leading during their long migration journeys.

As the seasons change, geese travel to find food, water, and safer nesting areas.

A group of flying geese can be called a skein.

Large flocks gather together before migration begins.

Cold weather and frozen ponds can signal that it is time to migrate.

Strong flight feathers help geese soar through changing weather.

Some Canada Geese migrate during the day, while others travel at night.

From sunrise to sunset, migrating geese continue their long journey.

Living Beside Humans

People sometimes feed geese in parks, but too much human food can be unhealthy for wild birds.

Parent geese may hiss or warn others when they feel their goslings are too close to danger, so it is important to keep a safe distance.

People may sometimes spot goslings exploring grassy areas near ponds and sidewalks.

DID YOU KNOW?

Some Canada Geese no longer migrate because they can find food year-round near humans.

Some geese become comfortable around humans.

People should always give wild geese space and respect.

Many Canada Geese now live in cities and suburbs throughout the year.

Parks, ponds, and grassy fields can provide good homes for geese.

Whether flying across the sky or swimming quietly on a pond, Canada Geese are an important part of nature.

The next time you see a Canada Goose, take a moment to watch and discover the wonderful world of wildlife around you.

www.ingramcontent.com/pod-product-compliance
Lightning Source LLC
LaVergne TN
LVHW080039170826
845677LV00025B/1469

* 9 7 9 8 9 0 3 5 9 0 0 6 3 *